Bread & Butter

like
no
other

SAEED
RAHMAN

ISBN: 978-1-7354115-1-4

Forever grateful
I am
For those of you
Who have valued
Copyright laws
And acquired this
Art
Through authorized mediums.
Copyrights give
Artists a path
To feel entitled to their
Creation
Without
Worrying about
Betrayal.

Author:
www.kalosynii.com
@saeedrahmann
@sublimekindness_

Artist:
www.sarahaladayleh.com
@s.adayleh

Bread & Butter:

To those who have nurtured me into life
Nadia Naz & Mashood Rahman
I may have not been the ideal child
But you were far more than the ideal parents
I am—because of your struggle and patience,
Shukria.

&

To the joys of my life
Shafiq Rahman—Bro
Azeem Rahman—Moni
Ohood Naz—Barbie
You are the pieces of my life
That make me whole.

———

The Pieces:

The Letter to you

The Falling

The Dwelling

The pains of Leaving

The warmth of Loving

The Meaning behind

To All those
Who I could Never understand
&
To All those

Who never Understood me

Dear lover,

Loving can be quite difficult. I think everyone who has ever
tried comes across some kind of pain—be it from a distance or
from choice. I may never have the answers to why people love
and leave the way they do, but I hope to one day understand
the pain they put us through. You are here, holding the skins
of a bark, reading rhymes of an art, hoping to find some
distant remedy in these pieced out melodies. You'll find words
that relate, words that anger, and words that leave you without
meaning—but you'll grasp through pages wondering if there
are others like you going through the same feeling. Because it
might be a boy that's troubling you in the back of your mind, a
girl that's left you way far behind—or a soul that has confused
you all through time…though, the fact remains that loving can
be a thrill unmatched, a feeling that has left your heart
unconditionally patched. These words are written not only for
the purpose of my heart's dismissal but also to ease yours that
has crippled.

It will always be an awe
To wonder
How something as simple
As bread and butter
Can taste
Like no other.

Perhaps a single request of mine would be to hum the words
you read further below—and think of the ones you will never
let go.

Here we go again—My insides whispered as my pulse began to rhyme.

The Falling

I have not known the taste
Of comfort
Until I shared a meal with you

Even bread and butter
Tasted sweeter right after kissing you.

B&B—

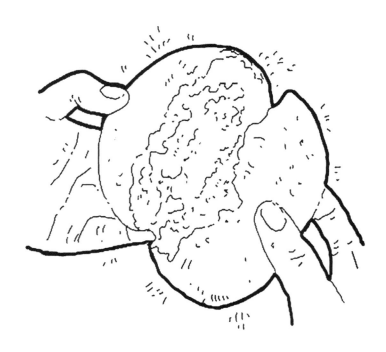

How could I want anything more
Than the loaf that loves to sit on my tongue

Cut in a slice

With nothing more than the glaze of butter
Dripping into the pores of that baked pillow.

I liked simple taste,
Like soft corner bread—

How could I have not realized you were
A different kind,

A kneaded beauty
Layered into a French diamond
Far from simple
          too close
                    to unexplainable

A taste I could not get over.

—Viennoiserie

Your face…too precious
                    For my eyes to gawk
My arms…too jealous
                    Of your jacket in March
Your body…too distant
                    For my skin to touch
My soul unworthy
                    Of the love you brought

You—

She is angelic…
Like Gabriel?

No.
But like the devil once was

—

I could look at you
With the same eyes

That once saw a rainbow stretch its ends
On different continents

I could look at you
With the same eyes

That bathed underneath the raging blue
Of a burning comet

I could look at you
Past all the wonders

And still be in awe

At how the colors of the curve in the sky
Could not compare,
To the soft red spawned on your lips

&

How the burning blue in the sky
Could not burn
Brighter than the blue in your eyes...

I could look at you
                    & never feel the need
                                    to look away.

But. I can't.

Look at you—

The shallows
The shells

Is somewhere I'd walk over
Without knowing too much
Of the deep.

By the time I swim over
I would be too tired to make it back
To the beach.

—To drown in you

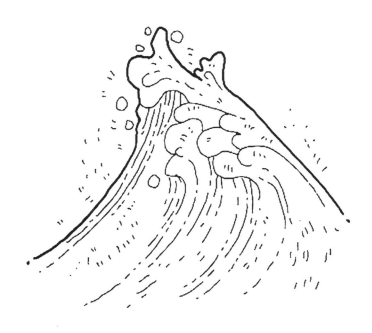

I hated chocolate,
You made brownies

That was the first time we met…
And I can't remember tasting anything sweeter,

That was after kissing you.

Brownies—

You are a compiled fascination
Of all the wonder
I want from this world.

—

Need me
Like how you
Kneaded toughened dough
Not from flowers
But the flour of dried snow
Sugar,
For some sweetness
And a pinch of hope
Then separate me into pieces
But keep me close
In the same palms
Of those hands
That molded me before
So please will you have me all
Before parts of me
Begin to mold.

—Baker

You were sitting on the sofa
And I made fun of your curls

It's strange because I remember
Every. Subtle. Twirl.

—That's when I fell

It only takes a while
To fall over
A glimpse of a smile
And I'm hungover

No need for the wine
Or the breadsticks

I think I'm full
From your eyes
And your fragrance

The smell of rose
On your skin
Like hard brandy

Makes me melt
From inside
Like caramel candy...

Drunk sugar rush—

Fly me to the river
Fly me past the moon

Show me how you dance
On a Sunday afternoon

I'll watch you spin around
Under a cloud laced with blue

It'll only be a while
Until the sun begins to drool

So, take me by the hand
And guide me where you move

Lead me past the skies
To escape this afternoon...

—

Times are getting lonesome, but I see you succeed
Days are getting colder, but I need not plead
The silence nor sorrow of an empty life;
And the constant glare of our ongoing strife.

I need not say the heart is weary;
But I'd rather perish than to see you demise.
Please oh please in birth do not disguise,
Your sorrow in rum and in tears you deny.

Never shall thou give up that elegant smile,
For a lady "oh so grown into perfection"
Be patient and still, as joy shall arise;
Within the beauty of your untouched complexion.

Doubt—

Christmas candy
Buttered brandy

It's nice to be home again

Winter snowfall
Silken overalls

I need to be held like
            Something to abstain

Sin in my voice
Gin on your breath

Let's make the devil
            drool again

—Christmas

Coffee in my palms
Sweater on my skin
Fire in my eyes
I'll find peace within

Cherry on my lips
Your hands running down my hips
Tell me all those lies
I'll pretend they don't exist

I'm burnin all the lust
In this coldended winter-fall
Your breath is all I need
Trust me I'll bare it all

Coffee—

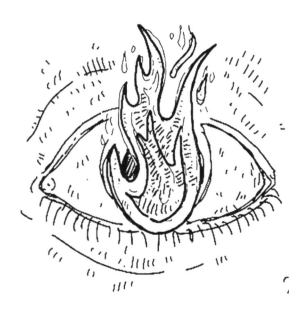

I can't help but feel
Infatuated
Simply by thinking of you.

—Thought

I hope this does not
Hurt

Like the others
before

Falling—

It becomes ultimately difficult
To explain what happened at first sight

And
Nearly impossible
To explain how...

—More than like

You should know
Loving is a fickle thing

Many call it a game
Some call it a chase

Few ever call it for what it is

Love I think—

Your laughter I suppose is
The one thing my mind
Can melodiously sway to

—Repeat

Your humor
Covers more of you
Than the skin your body
Stretches in

Hiding—

I told myself I would not fall again
What a lie that was

—

You are the sip of tea
That never loses its
Touch of warmth

—

I'm sorry you said after I kissed you
I felt your heart panic and your voice simmer
Why are you sorry? I asked

Your silence showed more of you
Than words ever could

—That one time

You felt like the right
Kind of exciting—

A borderline beautification
Of the calming chaos
Brewing in the back
Of my mind

—

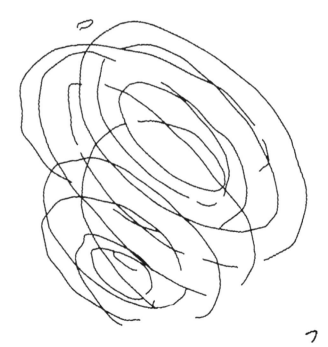

*I'm terrible at thi*s I said in hidden sweat
I'm pretty bad at this too you said
So…Friday?

—Best day of my life

I will never know
Why you hide
That soft side
Underneath layers
Of so much humor

You think I can't see
The enigma behind
Your need to laugh
Over
Your fear to fall

——Over

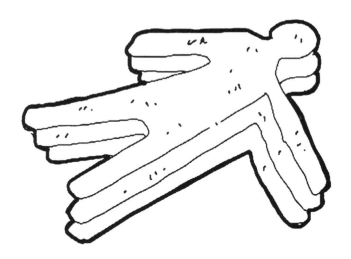

These people around
I will never forget
Like an extension of family
From different shades of red

—Friends

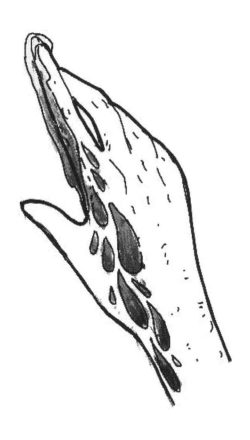

I could never like a movie
Without seeing it

I could never love a book
Without reading it

I could never admire a song
Without hearing it

Yet,
I have fallen for a soul
Without feeling it.

Existence—

Some don't know how to love
Some don't know how to heal
And some still
Unsure on how to feel

—

You were the flower forest
Pollinating the dunes
Of my desert den

Mirage—

If time did not exist

I would have sat and spoken
To you
For forever

—Streetlights

I wanted to hear you
Before ever laying my hands
On you
Wanted to see you
Long before wanting
To mark your lips

You made me listen to my soul
When the voices around
Made me believe
Boys
Could never
Live for love

How I was raised—-

That smile you try to
Hide when she comes
Within your peripheral

The work of magic it is—
The work of divine it is—

That simply her presence
In color
Can bubble a concoction
Of emotion
And leave time
So out of touch

—

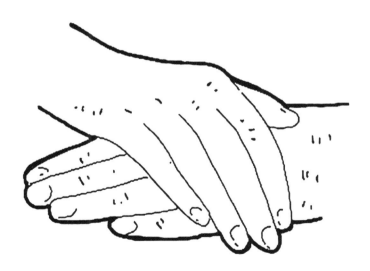

I hope one day
You see the
Exquisite existence
Of the woman you are

Worth—

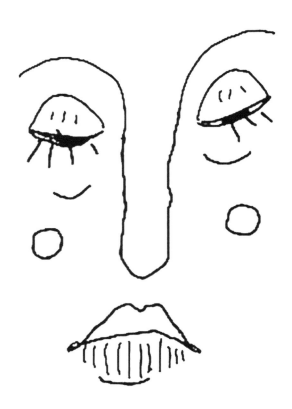

What is it about her They asked
What isn't I smiled back

—

Your hair was thick
A kind of forest
I didn't mind
Losing myself in

—

Fuck the *French*
Kiss me with your
Arabian nature

—

39

The other half that is spoken of
Is what I know I saw in you

That constant dance with
I can't love
Or
I don't want to love

Was just your fear of
Hiding from the truth

—

Your red lips on mine
Were the melting wax
That sealed the letter
Of my fate

—The mating soul

Wait—
Let me see you close.
Close enough
So you can take off all your clothes

Leaving me breathless
So speechless

No words.
Just my actions
On your skin

Like warm butter on
Hot bread.
Melting as it touches

Those hot pores
Of that soft soul
Blanket on your silk

Love wait—
Let me see you close—
Close enough
So I can
            truly have you all

—

Before you
I wished my life were different

I wished for a different city
Wished for a life away
From the old
And the busy

But now
That I am leaving

It is a sad to say
That some wishes come true
In an untimely setting.

—Queued

Give my lips a try and
Brace for a nightly
Aching

Guide my fingers south
And fulfill your
Wishful
Thinking

It might take a while
But don't you worry
This is just love
In the
Making

All-nighter—

The warming curves
Between our bellies
Reminds me of warm
Baked bread

That
I'll bite without breaking
Make you squirm
Without aching

Then—
Your kiss
Like no other
A melted sweet butter
On a searing skillet

—Breakfast in bed

You understand me so well
Almost feels like
You held my hand
While I traced through
The moments
Of my earthly hell

Co-author—

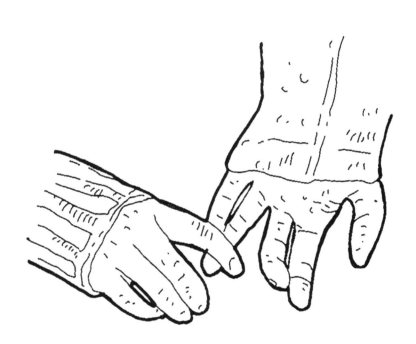

I get lost
In the nightly ocean

In the dark skies
And random constellations

With my brown eyes
And wild imagination

I reach the sky
And trace the curves
Of the faint light
Of stars in motion

I was stargazing
Not in the sky
But to my side

In the thick abyss
Surrounded by your
Ocean-blue iris

Stranded
Like an island universe

—

The blue in your eyes
Takes over me

Like the cascading waves
On the ocean floor

They reach into my soul
Like the currents bringing
Ancient shells
Onto the sandy shore

—

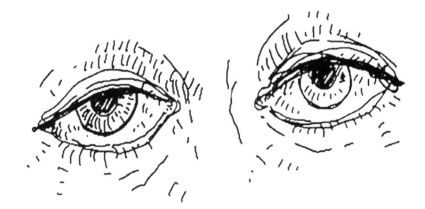

Whisper sweet nothings
Onto my lip
And watch me quiver
Under my hip

—Silent night

Caress the rain off
My shoulder blades
Or watch it trickle down
To a place
Where you'd find
A pouring river
Of your own doing

A mess of mine—

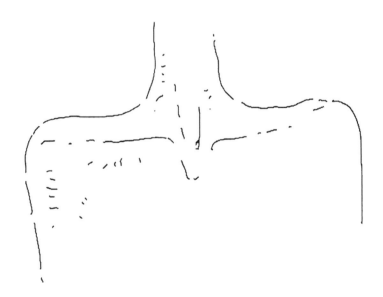

You are
A cactus
Who
Fends off thirst

With its spine on
The outsides

Afraid of
Its tender insides

Being sucked dry
By Bedouins
Who
Leave you
Out to die

—Your love for cacti

But little did you know
I was that summer rain
Feeding
Into your roots

A different kind of thirst—

I often
Ever feel
But when I do

The feeling is
Quite surreal

—

That coffee shop
Window we stared out of

Had a small reflection of two

You were busy people watching
While I was busy watching you

People watching—

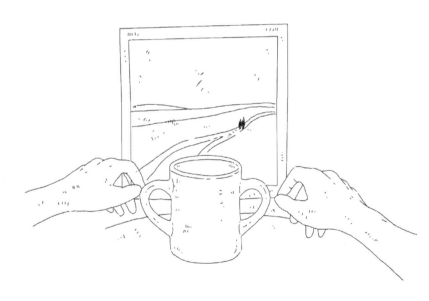

It was only when I saw you
That I knew
What I was waiting for

—

Your lips
A pristine nectar
I crave
To soothe the quickening
Pace of my heart

—

Heard you laugh
And saw you smile

Fall…

—my mind echoed

Never go looking for love, as the feeling itself does not know where it's hiding.

—

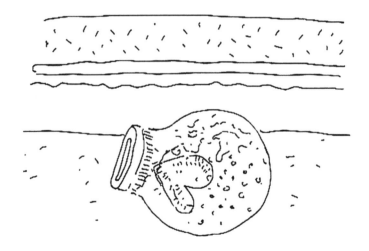

The
Dwelling

You told me
    I was bad
    Before I ever got
            Any good

——

Let's hitchhike to Heaven
And pretend
Hell does not exist.

Hitchhike—

The first time
        I left for heaven
Was the last time
        I saw the face of the earth.

—Afterlife

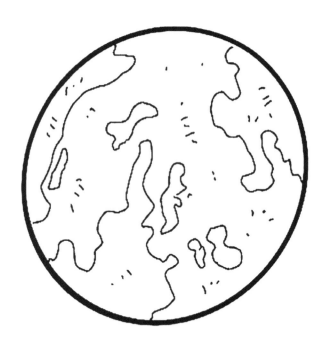

He mapped my skin
Like the ocean's surface

But forgot that every soul

Lies in the
            Deep.

Surface—

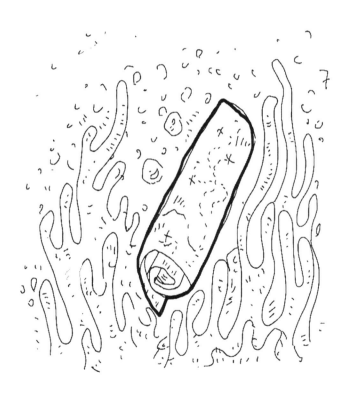

Down time
I need some down time

To think of you
While I sway
In my swivel chair

Down time
I need some down time

To wait and see
When I will
Move out of here

When all I wish
Is to disappear
Into the unknowns of all
That I will never know

About all of you
I will never feel
                                again...

—Down time

He said I'd be fine if I kept calm
Told me three words
As if I were looking for alms

His eyes gleamed joy
While mine screamed agony

I noticed his pleasure
But he didn't notice my pain

Is it my fault to have been so quiet
Or is it his to have been so one-sided

Pain—

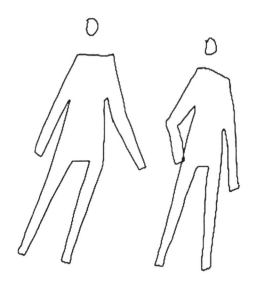

Can the ocean feel the touch of rain,
Like her skin on a cloudy day

Does it beckon the gentle trickle,
That glides down her slender neck

Oh! The sound of thunder,
The cry of nature
To feel oneself

Clouds above,
Oceans below,
And between
          A lovers end.

—Rain

It is a risk falling for another
Can't be sure if it's love
Or obsession that has taken over

Risk—

To feel estranged
I need not the feeling of lives
Instead, to seek the meaning of life.

But, that too, is overdone
To a point of hopelessness.

For questions too big to answer;
For feelings too large to explain,

I was told
        Ignorance
                Is the only remedy.

For I will wake at 6,
To look at screens till 9.

Glaring at night,
    Shimmering stars,
        Wondering,
           Is this the only therapy?

—Ignorance

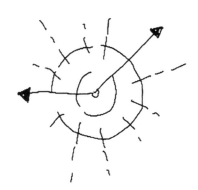

I was
Guided by a little light
        But
        Blinded by too much of it.

Light—

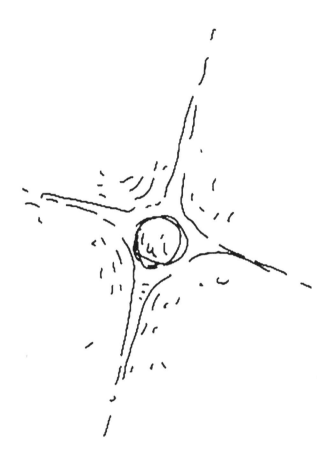

You slipped past me
Like water
In oil

Together
But alone

Hovering between spaces
Left wondering
How you were
All gone

—

So much chaos in you
Burns from the fear of your past

—

You are left wandering
When you have
Nothing left
To believe in

—

The heart
And
The mind
Seem to be at odds
Most of the time

Diatribe—

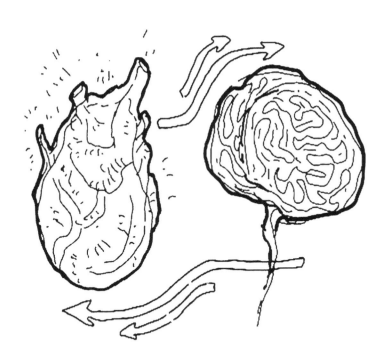

It would be nice to know
If she's thinking of me

—Everyone

There's this emptiness
I can't quite explain

Like one morning
My arms
Grew legs
And ran away

—

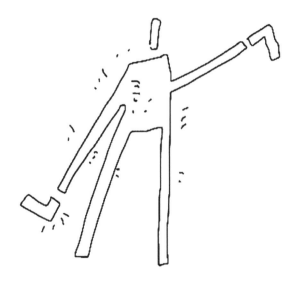

The not knowing why
Is a question we must all learn
To live with

—Another Mystery

Mother had never told me
Loving would be so hard

But
She had told me something
About the hurting

A wooden spoon—

Traditionally
Marriage is set
By those who have birthed
Not by those who have lived

And the first time they
See each other is on the first
Night of the bleeding

I guess they got the wrong idea
Of love
At first
Sight

—Romeo not Juliet

There are factions at home
The faction of my mother
And that of my father

One who understood but
Was never easy to talk to

One who was easy to talk to
But never understood

A give and take
Too difficult to learn from

Communication error—

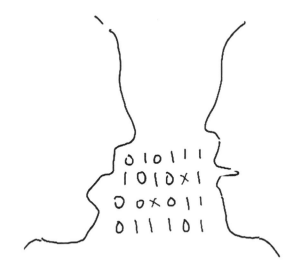

I was at a place I cannot recall
With people I no longer know
Chugging a drink, I could not taste

Pushing into a body I could not feel

—My first time

I wonder why we meet
The people we meet

A cosmic meaning
I hope
And not just a
Fluke of life

—

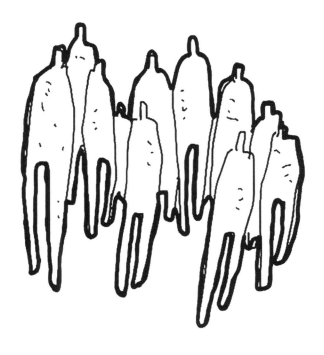

Why do I feel a bit empty
When I have lost none of myself
But all of you

—

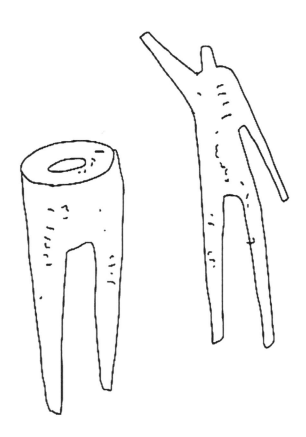

In all the years of life
It is strange to imagine
All the moments
In the making
That led me
To you

—

Time pass
Was what my mother
Called it when I told her
About being in love

I was nine then
A young believer
In cosmic disasters

—Brown

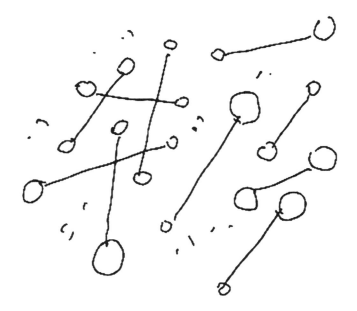

Under the starry night
Do you ever wonder
How many people
Have pointed up

Yet, looked
To the light
By their sides

I haven't either—

So many finding their other halves
Still, so many losing their only whole

—How I feel is somewhere below

I wake every morning
Hazy eyed
Staring into
The palm sized sun
Hoping one day
I wake to the bells
Of your
Written calling

Remember me—

Has no one ever questioned
How we can fall for someone
We had never knew existed up
Till the day they came about

—I'm sure everyone has

Why is it never simple
To be with those
Who took your breath away
And want them to be with you
Just the same

—

What was it about the time
We talked
That made you lose
All interest
In a soul
You once
Found
Bearable

—I hope not too much

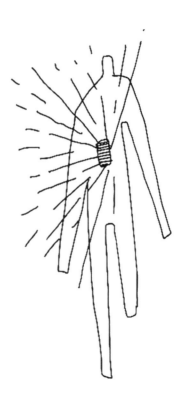

I don't like coffee too much
But drinking it with you
Made it easier to sip and stare

—

Arabian beauty
You have occupied
All the spaces in my mind

Your white pearl skin
And your ocean eyes
Your curly hair
And your scented highs

I could gush some more
But it would take a while

To finish up these words
And make you mine

—

I seem to fall
For the ones
That take
The longest
To get back
Up from

No not the stairs—

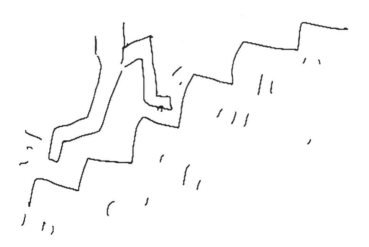

I never intended of feeling this way
I don't think anyone really does
It really just hits you out of nowhere
And you kinda have to hope
The other gets hit just the same

—

Often the softhearted
Are stepped over
To reach for those
Who are halfhearted

And then they ask why—

The lights are burning low
So,
Our hearts decide to slow

The rhythm begins to
Caresses my pulse

And your voice
Starts to show

A soft Winter loving
Away from the escaping Fall

And
It feels like forever
Since I've had you all

—To myself

I wonder
If there was a way
To make you stay
Without leaving you
                    Astray

—-

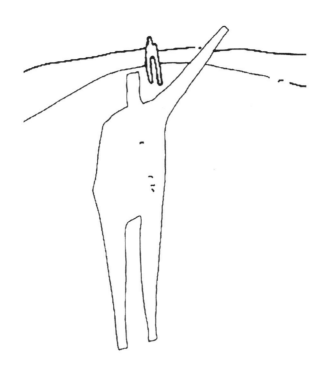

The stares
And
The glares

I could feed
Off your eyes
Live off
Your warmth
And never
Feel the need

To share a prayer
Oh, love…
Because,
I'd have you near

—To My Heart

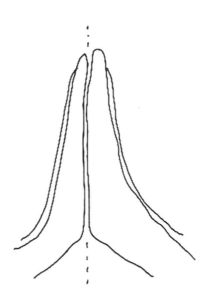

It's a shame one must hurt
In the pursuit of happiness

—

No
I was never
Taught how to love
Nor was I taught
What it meant to be happy

I was taught to be okay
Being pushed into a life
That I would blindly marry

—What a life

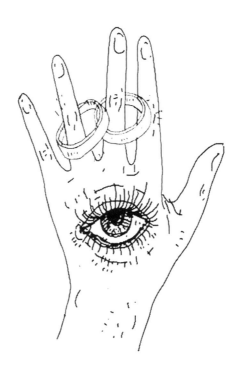

Don't you think they get lonely?
                    She asked
                         The stars in the sky...
          No,
               I said
                    They're brightening the sky for you and I

—

I'd call your name
In the wind
'Cuz it'd whisper it
In words
Nobody else would
Understand

—-

You said
Not to wait
But said nothing about
Hope

—-

Your peripheral
Catches mine
As you turn your head
I try not to stare
And wonder of a feeling
I can't define

—

Sweaters from the thrift store
Girl how you look so
Fine
In that ivory-blue

Take me to the coat
Aisle
Show me
How you find style
In the old and the new

No need for lipstick
Just a little nitpick
In the vintage after glow

None of the flashy
Away from all the classy
To clothes that they threw

I wonder how you pull off
The cottons they had enough of
You're still making them look
Like they're something more

I followed you in the store some
Walked by your side some
And all that you showed me
Was how much

You loved the thrift store—

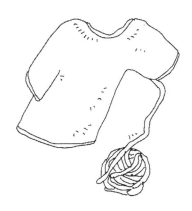

She was
Looking through some vinyl
Hoping she could find some
Indie that she knew

I was watching from her shoulder
Wanting to know more of
The wonder in my view

But all I could know was
She only had love for
The thrift store by the moon

—Still there

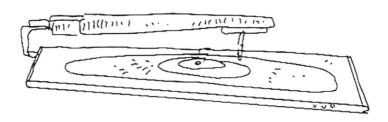

The walk back home
Was tiresome
So I stopped by the park

I looked around the apartment homes
And heard a little song
It was some distant melody
One that I could hum

Then,
I spotted a windowpane
One from the song
You once played to me

They were lovers
Hand in hand
Moving to notes
Of a band

And
I couldn't help
But
Wonder
If this is what
Love must look like

This love unplanned—-

Let's bathe
In the crystals
Of the night sky

A diamond dust
Underneath your tight eye

It would be like one of those
Galactic explosions
An umbrella
Under the heated tensions

Birthing
A Casanova
In the melting core
Of a ruby red

—Supernova

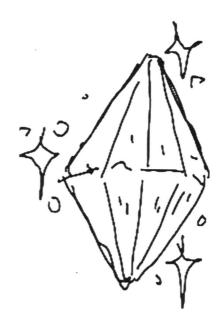

I find myself wondering a lot these days, he said
          can't seem to be moving any further

     Then start wandering instead, she said
          trust me further is all you'll ever want to go

Wanderer—

To those early dwellers, beware that

all it takes
is the smallest
of sparks to light
the wildest of fires

L*** on Fire——

The pains
of Leaving

How the hurting leaves me
Wanting to write more
Than the drugs I get high on
In closed doors

—Is a mystery of its own

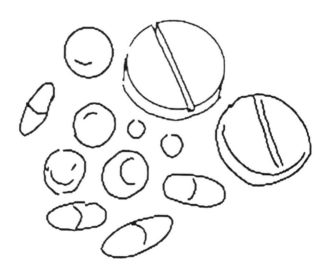

I stuffed my mouth
With all the food I could find

I looked up from the picture of you with another
Then I realized

I had the munchies of a different kind

High—

I eat when I'm high
I eat when I'm low

There is no getting around the pain
Of letting go...

—Still high

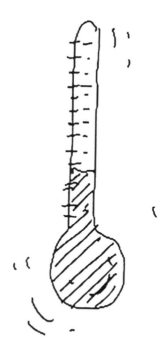

Boxes of cigarettes
Are melting away
With every puff
That I take
Because I'm
Feeling a bit on edge…

From all the memories
That you left me with
There's a hurting that
I seem to miss—
A haunting that
I can't ignore…

It's your voice
It's your smile
It's that awkwardness
That you couldn't find your way around…

But I still want you
After those twenty little chimneys
Burning their cores in my lungs.

And I'd still want you,
I'd even call out your name after
My voice has all but gone

—

I'm six feet away
From reaching your arms
From smelling your soft perfume.
I'm keeping that distance
From here to the moon
Because I can't lose you
When morning
                turns to noon.

It's not that easy
Staying home feeling queasy
In the confines of what seemed like home
Because there's a lot more to this distance
Than staring at your walls and the windows
And hoping it all goes away sometime soon.

Because I miss all those strangers
That I walked by on pavements
In the springtime or maybe in June
I miss being close to them
Without being afraid of those
Who might have the flu...

I don't want to think that way
Because I'd like the sun on my face
And the wind in my hair
And the voices of laughter
                in the blue,

—A World in my View

It'll always feel that way
When the sun sets down
And the clouds begin to take their form

You'll remember feeling more alone
In the silence of your home
Than in the crowded streets
                        of city stones

Those empty seconds
You never knew you had
Will make you think of more
Than you'd like to recall

Because we,
Don't like to share with
Those who are close

Because we,
Don't know how to put
Those thoughts into words

Not even me...
            Because I knew myself
                        Better when I was young.

Not too long ago—

The wanting
        Hurts more
                Than the waiting

—

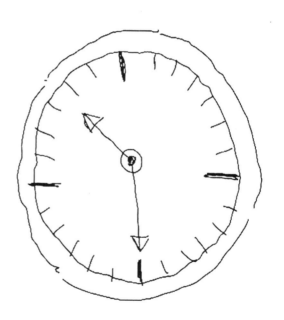

If she laughs at your kindness
Far from your presence
She is the one that does not know
The softhearted lover
The wildness undiscovered
She will never
            unearth

Missing out—

Their hearts do not bleed like yours
But how could you have seen
Through their thick skin…?

To you they were one and the same
A soul in space looking for gravity to hold on

You saw a world in the making
Without questioning
Where they came from
Because that never matters
When a heart
Bleeds love you can't contain

It wants them not
                    needs them
But it was too late to know then
                    what a shame…

They use all the gravity
Then
Leave you without any

And now you are floating
In space
Feeling so out
Of place

—

Peaceful are the Skies
When the clouds bring wind
And the air breathes warmth

Look at the orange sky turn purple
in the evening rain

And I will be there with an umbrella
holding back pouring pains.

Umbrella—

Little boys have no hearts
                    they say

Then why does it hurt so much
                    I sobbed

—

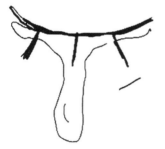

These strings on wood
are too tight to sound

Like his hands on her neck
to which she didn't consent

—

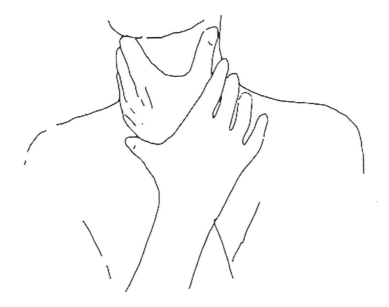

There is far too little
In the space of my trunk

With nothing more than the clothes
That warm my body

A few possessions I can't name
Because I couldn't care to find them a place

I think back—lately that is all I do
Because I care too much about the presence of people

Leaving me stranded in limbo
Sitting then standing
Then wondering, *what now?*

I have shifted homes like pairs of jeans
Felt it tighten around my thighs
To a level of comfort
But finding anew
As soon as it feels familiar.

Nomad she calls me
No ma'am—not mad I humor,
Just a little lost.

—Nomad

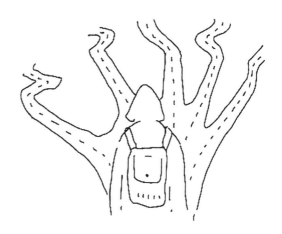

Home
They say it's
The *people* not the *place*
But what
Should I do when
They're trying to
Erase
A race
From knowing where
They once were from

Don't you know I'm human
Don't you know I feel it too
The pain
The misery
The replacing
Of history
Not fond of
Memory…

There are memories
That I have
Memories my parents
Do too
Of a coast in the west
That has shrunken
Way too fast

&

I thought you'd understand
Because you've
Been through pain
Under a similar hand

But I guess humanity
Never learns from cruelty
Of the past…

West Bank—

My soul misses you
Like how my body misses
The arms of a jacket
In the springtime

—

You got me used to all that coldness
Made me bundle in thick coats like Everest

Then moved on like the Winter snow
Leaving me stranded
          Away from
                    that springtime glow

—

Look around
Look away

Because I want to stay
In the past

Away
From all the future pains
Away
From all the blue dark days...

Look around
Look away

Because I want to stay
In your arms
Like a babe

Close enough
So I can
Hear your heartbeat...

—-

Don't look around
Don't look away

And leave me here
All alone

Because
I haven't got
All the time in the world,
Haven't got a heart made of stone.

—

I remember waking up
To a bag full of toys
Of the prehistoric era

And that would be enough
To make me smile
Enough to leave me
Happy
For a week—maybe two.

Now, all I can think in twenty-two
Is what I will be in forty-two.

Alone with nothing to do
Thinking of me and you.

—Toys

You made me doubt
That someone like me
Could ever be worth loving

A mistake of mine—

She was kind to me. A kind of kindness I did not want to forget because it seemed so good to me. That was the first time we met —you see. Out of the blue and completely blindsided, but there was more to her than the humor she basked in—in front of everyone. Perhaps that's my fault—for knowing too little and giving it all. Yet, I wanted her so…so much that I couldn't think at all. It still hurts to be—the one on the end that feels it all.

I don't want to find my other half
While losing my only whole.

—

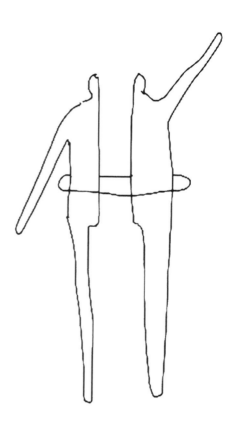

The sun seems to be giving up
It's been dark for too long

It could be the winter snow
The calm before the storm

I'd stand
        and
            I'd freeze

I'd beg
        and
            I'd plead

For the warmth on my knees
To start creeping up

Because,
        I'm not giving up.

—Winter

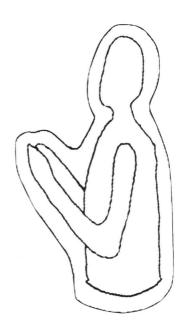

There is no quite feeling like love
Oh just you wait honey the cynic said
Then,
There was no quite feeling like loss

Cynical—

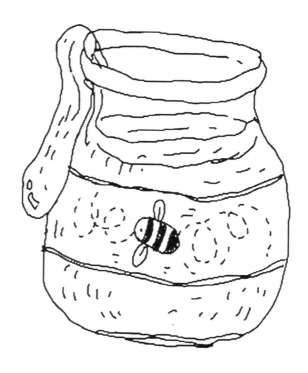

I wonder why I find myself with small white blankets
Is it for comfort or a spill from an old wine bottle
No, I don't think it's the latter,
I remembered to have drank it
On a long walk back home
With an awful lot of wobble

They're soft and light, like silky skin
And can blend on your cheeks, fixing a smile within

But I still wonder if it's big enough for each other
Because a bucket wouldn't even seem to fit,
The tears we'll shed when time will soon tick,
And love that'll near us to a quick smother.

So, I guess it's for comfort and I don't mean a slumber
That I carry these,
Much like your neck with a silver locket
For your tears I have kept,

—Tissues in my pocket

She was shy
For not too long

She was strong
For far too long

People took away her innocence
The world took away her arrogance

Still she walked straight
With a heavy smile

Knowing that it would take
More than a mile

Too long—

I looked out the window for some closure
Knowing, my mind couldn't close her.

She sounded like the roaring thunder
And felt like the brisk of mist.

She passed by like an olden stranger
And felt like the one I missed.

I could hear her make love to the ocean
While I walked around the deafness of a lake.

To hear her; symphonic.
        To see her; enigmatic.
            To feel her; euphoric.

—Senses

Is it wrong to never awaken
From the last sleep that I have taken

Is it wrong to wish to be lost in darkness
Rather than feel the warmth on the lid of my eyes

Because the space in my mind feels a lot freer
Than the steps on land they say are endless

Bound by borders that leaves me a number
I would rather spend life in a deep slumber

—

Shivers took the veins in my palms
Plaguing my body one strand at a time

I wish it was the cold that did such damage
But it was the mind that held such carnage

It was an endless hunger, not like a feast
It was an urged desire at the least

I plead to the sense of my remaining moral
Only to realize it was the dreadful withdrawal

—Addiction

I would wait
Even if
It meant
To see you walk away
In the hands
Of some other

I would wait
Even if
It meant
I would have
No other

I would wait
Because
My heart
Is too stubborn
To know
That it will one day
Never beat again.

Stubborn—

I want to walk
On the surface of Mars

Feel the cold air
Freeze my insides

I want to die
On some distant planet
And hope my soul
Doesn't inhabit

Another body in time
Just so I can
Live through
The same pain
Over and
          Over again

Take me to Mars
Where I can live out
My only days of
Satisfaction
And heartbreak

Maybe I could make a life out here
Maybe I could find a home out here
In the great red

—Unknown

Oh divine—
Heal my heart
As you would
My health

Because it's bleeding
In places
I can't
Defend

—

There is so much
I want to say to you

But every time
I open my mouth
I put an ocean of space
Between us two

—

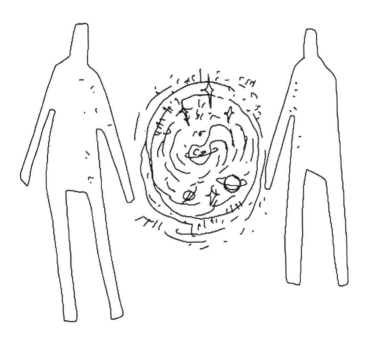

143

Honey water
Oh how
I want her
      A burning memorabilia
      In my palm

Sweet sensation
Thick fixation
      A numbing amnesia
      left behind

Gone—

You still have all of you   she said

Then why do I feel so halved?

　　　　　　　　　　　...

—

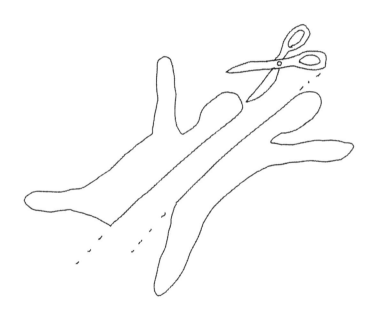

I become shapeless
In my molten shell

In that bubble of
Frustration
I let it boil
Till I can't take it

Then I take a deep breath
Let the ash suffocate my lungs

And only then I feel lighter
Only then I feel

Closer to the Clouds—

You took my kindness for humor
Wrung it out for cheap jokes at an ice breaker

Gave a gift away
Like an unenthusiastic charity goer
And then laughed some

No—please laugh some more
Keep it in your trunk and remember me
                              some more
Think of how it felt when I went encore
                                   on your lips
                    but let's be honest you thought it was
                                        shit
Because you flaked so fast that I almost missed
              your fear of movin so fast
                         and getting hit

But, *love*—I was only walkin by…
                    only walking along…

Never liked gifts——

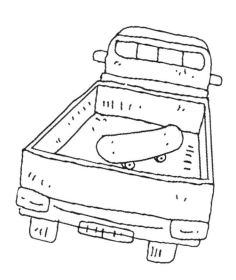

147

My bones
They're all but
giving in

Limb
By
Limb

And I know
The time
Is coming
Where I can't walk
on my own

I know
It's all about to end
Too soon
Before I've spent
Any time
With you

But it's fine
'Cuz now
I've got nothing left
To lose

—

I'd like to fish in the quiet
And catch no fish

Just a pole in my hand
With no live bait

The lake would be grey
And the skies would reflect

The breeze would be warm
And I'd have no regret

Of being so alone
So far from home

I'd look up at the sky
And whisper, *SOS*

Just of a different kind—

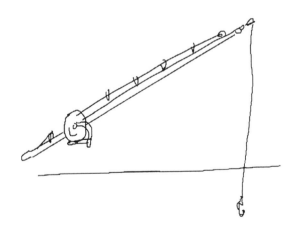

149

Rip into
My throat

Like a puff
And a smoke

I will breathe
You in
Like wrapped nicotine

I will cough
And I'll choke

Still I'd crave a little more
Till I'm high and I'm broke

In the night
When it's dark
And it's grey…

With nothing much
Left to say
'Cuz I'm choked up

On those dry empty tears
From those fake blissful cheers
From my mates past those years

And I'm sorry
I've fallen
       so low…

—Laced wafer

I am tired.

Tired of feeding
Into a feeling
That fades

My heart away...

—

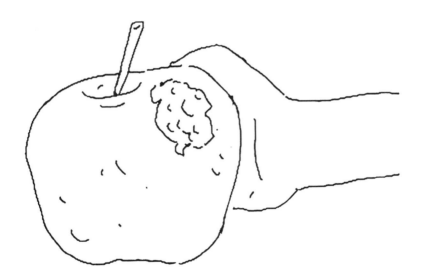

What's the point? He asked through a cigarette

    so you can know pain before the real thing comes along…
                   she said lighting it.

—Vaccine

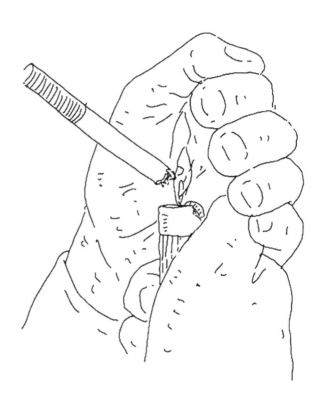

No medicine for the heartache
Just drugs for delirium
And a painful state of panic…

—-

You'll find the need to know
Why or
      what or
           when or
               how—

Please don't waste your time honey,

          it will be a while till you know.

—That one friend

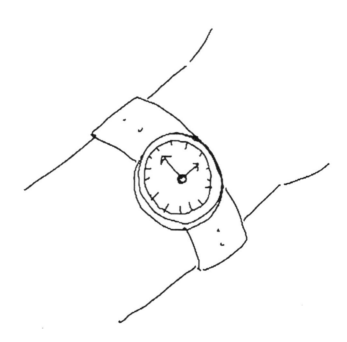

I want to find it.
That feeling of warmth—
Feeling of a soft heated blanket in the snow.

I want to hold it.
The crystals of a storm in the making
Large enough to take us whole.

I want to feel it.
Like your soft ember cheeks
On the aging crease of my palm.

I want you back now…
Like that one piece of shell
I lost in the shore.

No more—

I write to remember
I write to forget

It's a poetic mess
        I can't explain all too kindly
Because I'm a mess of a man
        I swear.

I've got that teeth clenching anger
That old scarring trauma
That love for being hurt again.

But, love—
        I want it.
Like a kitten in a casket
That was left out in a basket
When it was too cold for pulses
              to flow...
But, no
        I won't have it...

—Because it's the same Ohio-winter
            that I will forever know

Oh Mother
You let me stretch in your womb
But kept me locked in my room

Is this punishment for making you
Ache this long...

If it's pain that you're after
I'll wish I was never even born

But...
Maybe you care way too much
Of the world you have watched
And lost the meaning of what it means
To be whole

Oh Mother how can I tell you
That I am no longer that
            soft spoken soul

Spoken—

We'll get too old to wonder what went wrong
And settle for an unheard song
Convincing ourselves that this melody
Vibes with the melody of our soul—

Though,
It'd be like listening to a song
And not knowing where the beats belong
Because we'd end up swaying for far too long—

I hope my palm
Does not feel foreign
On the birth-marked map
Of your skin

Pisces in Pieces—

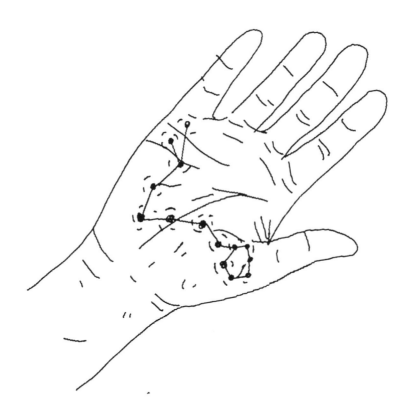

Never be too nice
　　　　　She said.
But, how can you ask a fish not to swim so freely?
　　　　　　　　　　　　I wondered.

—

I wasn't even looking
It sort of just hit me out of nowhere
Like those cars in New York City

While I was just jaywalking straight past your hair.

Tangled in your Curls—

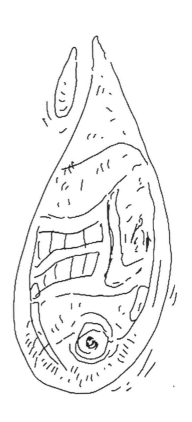

Always one-sided
Never wholehearted
It feels like forever till it gets anywhere

—

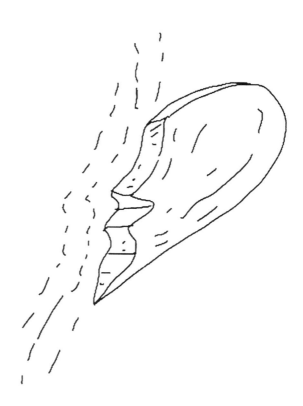

You've left me blinded
In a world where there's still
So much left to see

All the colors
They're greying
       not greening

Into a spectrum
Of palettes, where
       red has not much to be

Right now they're just feelings
       the uncertainty in shades
       is bottled into a shape

Of my mind that has been displaced...

———

I was once told that the life I live would not be

                                                  kind
                                                  to me,
                                                  that
                                                  it
                                                  would
                                                  bring
                                                  me
                                                  down
                                                  on
                                                  my
                                                  knees

                         they were right.

—Stand back up

The warmth
of Loving

Time
Will stand
The love that
Our hearts could not
Beat long enough to Feel

—

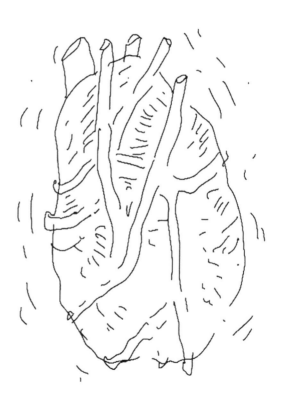

Why is the idea of mates in soul
So peculiar to some—

Is it so hard to believe
That you can love
In a glance of one

—First sight

It is in your
Kindest nature
To love thyself

—

You always worried
About where I was in the AM

On the sofa next to the door
Is where I'd find you waiting

Did you eat…?
      Are you hungry…?
          Let me make you something real quick
          You'd say with your sleep unhurried

I was young, hot headed, with anger slowly escaping
But it was only later that I knew
      It was unconditional caring…

Now, I am older
Still you seem to be hating
The space
Life has put between
You and I
That—
I know
Is daunting…

But never can I
Forget the days
I found you praying
On the rug
Next to God
In the morning
That was blinding

I'd curl
      into a ball
          next to your knees
              and hear your prayers
                  in whispering

Mother, your words are my summer
          in the endless cold
             of a world
                in the making…

Hope—

I'm getting older
With the motion of time

They say it's a sickness
From above, the divine

It'll take us all
Whether in youth or in prime

There's no running
From the pressure on my spine

Even Evil knows
When to hide from the signs

So, I stay gracious
With Kindness,
                    Sublime

—

It is a little difficult to say how much
I love you
Perhaps it is cuz I am a boy
Not like how I say it to her
Perhaps it is 'cuz she's the one
Who gave me life

I don't know how I should tell you that
The laughs you gave me are my only joy
I call you to ask
How you make the foods
You once used to make
In a house I once called home

Was it a pinch of red chili
With some ginger…
A cup of oil and
And masala

Recipes that I really wanna
Keep in enclosed in my little void
I could look through them
A hundred times
But I'll still call to hear your voice

Some oil…
Some onions…
Medium heat on the stove…
I'll cook and cook and show you how
No matter the times I replicate
Nothing ever tastes as good as yours
Cuz they're missing your hands
A presence I adore

You'll smile and tell me that it looks *alright*
I'll watch and wonder when I will be left behind
To open the void of recipes all alone

And perhaps It will be the day I finally tell you so,
That father I am still your little boy…

Recipes—

I am alive
But, not yet Living
In the space of my mind
That I find fitting,

It is the price one pays
To settle for that which is blinding.

Then,

Do what you must
To find
What is binding,

A life of bliss
In the depressing abyss
Of reality unfolded
Into a space you will not miss.

Become what you fear,
Breathe what is near
The suffocating cloud of uncertainty

From that you'll arise,
A soul oversized
Reaching for the stars
With more than just your sanity.

—-

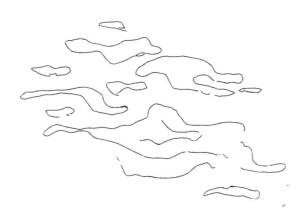

Have you heard the one
Where people say
She wasn't really the one
         or the one that goes
                  Plenty of fish in the sea...

Yes—aren't we tired of hearing those
                  sugar coated epiphanies
                           Where all we can do is nod and smile
                                    and hope we don't drown
                                    till we come by a fish
                                    that does not swim away...

—

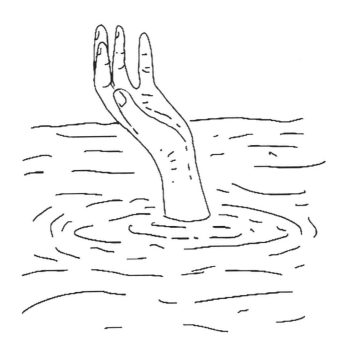

You'll know it when it comes
That nervousness in your fingers
The glances you can't get enough of
The walking you to your car because
Damn you look good in that midnight glow

It'll come to you
and
I hope you're not too afraid of saying okay
because love is as strong as it is fragile in its bond.

—

Love
Is not too fond
Of time and space

—Unstable

You're a wild star
Zipping through the blank skies
Waiting to get latched on
By my open hands

—

How much do you believe?
     She said with her thumb anchoring my lip
A lot more than I should…
     I looked at her hoping she would stay till
                  —next evening

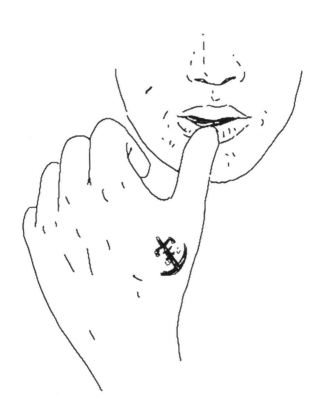

Mon Chéri,
      your tongue whispers words
                far too foreign
                      to make off…
Oh Cherry,
      Your lips infuse a taste
               far too sweet
            …not to get rushed on.

Sugar rushin'—

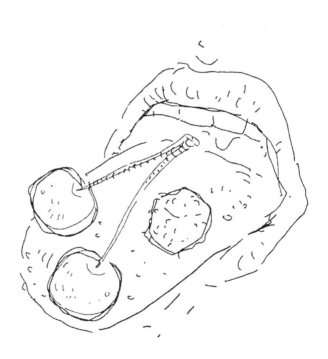

Coffee?
       no—Tea, please

Lemon?
       no—Lime, please

Sugar?
       no—your lips my dear

Some heat?
       no—just hold me near

Time?...
       nothing for that
               it's clear

—Substitute

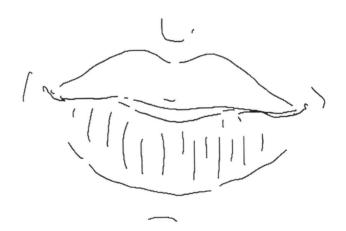

I want summer lovin
In the winter snow

Those morning whispers
In the sunlit glow

I couldn't ask for more, love
Because it's all I know

To love so wildly
         that in the end there's
         nothing much left
         to show

—

You want her to want you
The same way
Your heart does
      but get lost in the way
      that she treats you
      in the first half

Don't you know there's more to love
Than that sweet honeymoon Fa-cation*
A time where everything seems
Like an early celebration

So do yourself a favor, honey
Keep your eyes from being runny

Chin up
Chest out
Don't look
      like you're stressed out

Because eight billion people
                and some
Are looking over their shoulders for love
               just minus one…

—

No—they don't really teach you
How to love yourself

    Because they want you to buy
    Those clothes you didn't ask for

        Style yourself in some shades
        With some makeup that powders
        Your face

            You're just masking your glow
            Attracting some lows

            And wondering why
            Love never showed

            —

—

But it's been there
All along
In the bathroom at home
Reflecting back while
You brushed your teeth

    That face you wake up with
    Every morning
    That face you stare at
    As you're crying
    That laugh you can't see
    But feel…

        It's always been there
        Looking out while
        You were scared

            A beating right under
            Your chest

            A reflection that knows you
                the best—

Let's clarify
Your best intention

And deny your inhibition
For the night…

'Cuz it's an exhibition for
The lovely Extradition
Of those brutal love infections

That gave no reciprocation
no—not even for a second

Because all they ever wanted
Was to know that they were wanted
By someone other than a soul they called their own

—Insecure

They unwrap you and toss you
Like calories of uneaten chocolate
Just to feel satisfaction from the look
In their eyes…

Wrapper—

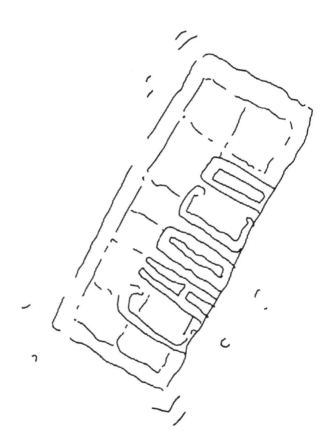

They will hurt
You will heal

It is only a matter of time
Till you feel

—Again

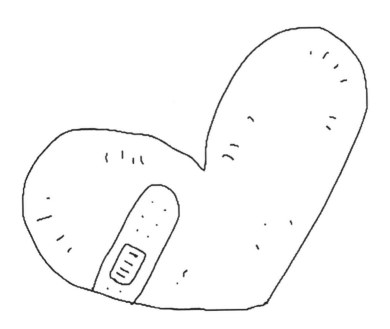

Loving.

It is a way
Your heart
Whispers so quietly
Which you will
Speak into words
          ever so loudly

—

There is no way I can
Remove you from my existence

You have already sunk your softness
In the ridges of my past tense

—

It is only ever complicated
As you ever make it

Or them—

You will often crumble
At the subtle sounds of her name
Even melt at the familiarity of her voice
And *oh*, will it be known when you see her face
Because she will not be a desire you crave at dawn
Nor a hunger that burns from the southern midlands

She will be the missing pitch in your laughter
The helping hand you long chased after
The lost thoughts that let you wander
She will be anything and everything
                        that makes you feel whole...

—

Moving away is a part of life
That no one seems to talk about
I guess it's because no one knows
A whole lot about what it means to
Let go of something
                    someplace
                              someone
                                        or
                                        somemany

Because no-one ever actually wants to move on
And look ahead of memories they will now make
Because,
They're all stuck in memories that they already made

It's always like that—

Now that I've got you thinking about what it means to leave the familiar—know that I was where you are or I am where you are...In a place where I don't know the people around or people beside—they are all just bodies vibing in a space they created and blocked out—or so you think till you finally find the courage to take that step out and voice that soft-spoken *hello...will they hear me?...will they laugh?...will I ever be enough?...*I don't have a miracle cure for feeling so alive that will push you past that border of comfort—that is what the alcohol and headache is for...I can't simply tell you to love yourself so deeply that you feel this high of deliverance—a freedom from inside that lifts that soft-spoken *hello* into a bellowing HOW YOU DOIN....because it is not as simple as seeing yourself in true light. You've been doing that every time you put on a shirt and check yourself out in a mirror of some mall store...you have to know that moving away is not moving on—it is growing...it is knowing enough to live through all the feelings...that place you once ate at is most likely going to be around, still selling that coffee with some hazel, cookie with some raisins—and you'll look back wanting to know if there were any stores out there in the world that ever offered some tea with an angel...

—Guess you'll never know until you go

Asking you to see me
The same way
I see you

Would be like asking the blind
To keep their eyes wide open

—

You're like that cup of tea
In the morning waiting to be sipped

Warm bodies
Cold sorries
We're kissing but
                was I really missed...?

—Distance

Friends they tell me
That happiness
Will come for everyone

But they don't know
I have found it
In that only one

—

Crystalize
Crystal eyes

I've stared so much
You made me
Realize
Real eyes

Not to look too hard
They just might be
Poisonous
Poison mess

I've gotten so used to
That
loneliness
lovelessness

I want so much more
but my mind
has all but
repressed

—

It is much like that song
You once heard
And forgot about

Then one day
Remembered a little hum.

You scrolled
Through playlists
Wondering where it
Could have gone around

Then spotted an
An artwork
Deep down.

A sound—a smile—a feeling
                              profound

You tap
          and wait
                    then hear it all around

The strums—the strings—the melodies
                                        in-between

You see a face
              and your pulse
                            causes a scene

A moment in song you couldn't do without
                            a memory in mind
                                        you couldn't live
                                                without…

Those memories I had at nineteen—

I have loved you
Like I have loved
The feeling of bread

Soft and tender
Warm and splendor
Then drowned under all
                    the regret

—-

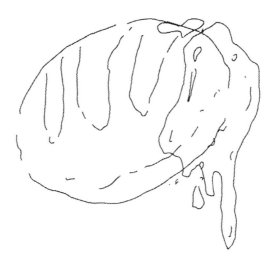

You will want to tell them what is on your mind. You will want to tell them everything—in fact there will be times you almost do. There will be times you actually do—those will be the times you feel like you shouldn't have just because they were not ready or were too unfamiliar with what it means to be loved. They were tried with the halfhearted, whole asshole—ish romantic tussle and left with a heart that wants nothing more than to hustle—not for love that remains but a feeling that escapes. They want that *leave me* loving with the *hurt me* bluffing and a side piece kept on reserve. Everyone seems to want that warm fuzzy feeling but get too scared of the friction. It makes you want to take that step back—it makes you want to backtrack on ever feeling loved. Makes you want to cut back on ever being heard. But love is a feeling unknown—love is a dive into the deep without the light reaching around your peripheral—love is like when the blind take steps without a cane because they feel the presence of that corner-piece. Just because you have been let down a few does not mean your heart will not repair—it is a muscle that takes the longest to heal because it is an engine that feeds your mind, body and soul without crying

    unfair...

—

I wanted to love
Like how
          butter
Dissolves
On the surface of
          bread
A tempting golden
Drooling on the pores of
Of your soft skin

—Sweet & Salty Resemblance

You are the kind of sweet
I would not mind gaining weight from

The exquisite appeal
They'd fly over New York for

A delicacy
        my heart craves more than
                my tongue does

Because there's not one like you
That gets my pulse rushed like your buzz

A thick taste on my tongue
                like Kanafeh—

There is more
Than just
The ocean in your
                eyes

There is water from heaven
                pouring rain
                from the sky

Tides so foreign
                a force
                I can't simplify

A green
                so blue
                it leaves me
                        mystified——-

You mold me
Much like the sheets
Of warm pastry—

A shape I can no longer
                              outgrow
—

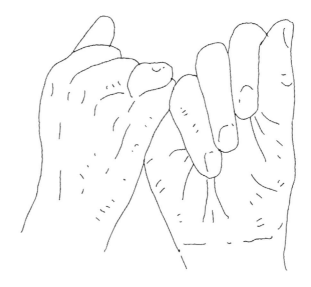

I often remember
The way you left
It makes me wonder
why

All while knowing
    how you came
    was a mystery
    just the same

—

It is highly
Unlikely that I will
Find another mind that
Thinks the way I do
But the best way
To get by is
Knowing
When to
Lose

—

You are the kind of craving
That can never be quenched

—

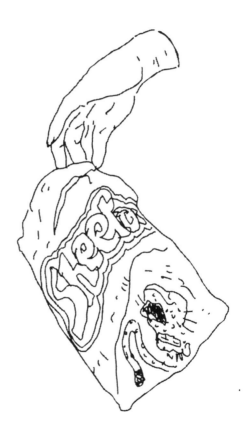

My love,
The pain you feel
Makes itself known
So gravely
That it seems like
It will never go away
But time will try
Its best to hide
That pain under years
Of some divine destiny

—

You have lost
Not your life
But a piece you thought
Would make you whole

Love,
  Don't you realize
  The heart you have
    Has always been your home?

—

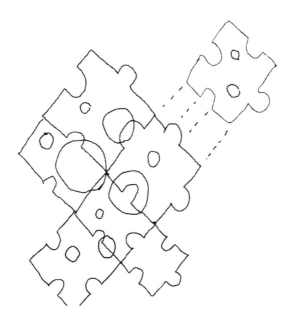

Poetry
&
I
Have
Never
Been
Fond

but
It
Is
What
I
Needed
Most
To
Feel
Loved—

Love yourself
So graciously
That others
Feel tempted
To learn

—

These words
Of kindness
I hope were
Not too blunt
To hurt
The wound that's left
Astray

There's love
There's loss
And an ocean
          across

Of souls waiting to be frayed.

—

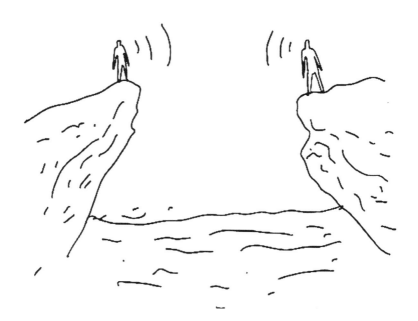

Inexplainable
Like ancient letters
I can't recreate

It's like being cornered
In a room without space
Basking in the dark,
            hoping to dissipate

Like suffocating on your own words
Out of the sheer pain of not being understood
Just because that feeling is so unique to you that—*No*
No one can understand your pain, no one can relate to it
But, they can—and you want that loneliness with a safety-net

A rope in your hand so they can understand
                        your pain in every alphabet
Of intangible emotions radiating off of you like an astronaut
                        slipping out of a safety vest

That pain. That struggle. Of not knowing where you'll be or
                who you'll be in the long pause of a
                                        calculus test.
But, wait—Life's a pyramid. It goes up and down
            —Life's magnanimous. So, breathe and take it slow
                                because in a
                                while you'll be
                                a lot more
                                than the rest
                                of us.

Pyramid—

I am satiated
From eating too much bread
But my heart still beckons to one day
Be quenched.

You have stayed till the end, and perhaps
That may be enough
To keep me happy
Till my stomach begins
To crave what my heart
Has long been lacking.

—To you,

Shukria...

Bread
&
Butter
like no other
Is a collection of words
That sum up the stages of
Falling into
A feeling so
Familiar
yet so
Foreign.
From the initial fall
To thoughts that
Have taken you all,
To the broken
Pains
Of never
Again…
It is a piece that reminds
Us of how we feel
And how one should never
Feel discouraged
Of loving again—
Even if it means
To revisit the times
That have left you damaged.
Know that loving comes from within
And so does pain—
The longer it is held onto
The longer it will resonate.
So, comfort your hearts
With the feeling unknown
And know that your
Heart will heal
For as long as you
Give it the chance
To feel—

—You all

like no other.

Now, after pages of poetry it seems almost impossible to hush away the rhymes and get back to the natural times. But, before you flip me close and keep me aside like a wilting rose, I'd like to let you know that there are people in this world that I couldn't simply do without.

Amina Al-Araji
Rabab Al-Araji
Mohammed Bahaeddin
Aseel Al Adayleh
Heba Al Adayleh
Abdullah Ziyad
Saniya Mansoor
Parth Tiwari
Aisha Moin
Asma E. Saleh
Mishgan Abdullah
Mechail Haswani
Sandra Haswani
Sara Al-Nimer

& Sarah Al Adayleh, without whom these words would feel incomplete.

Thank you for simply…being.

———

SAEED RAHMAN—born in the KSA, and tossed around the Middle East like an old duffle bag patched with scotch tape. I could've gone on in third person, but it only seemed right to tell you a bit more about myself…as myself. Moving can be a fickle thing, especially when you're asked the unanswerable question, *"where are you from?"* Well, to put it simply, I am not sure. By blood, I am Pakistani. By the figurative time and length of stay (to date), I am Middle Eastern. However, I've roamed the areal continent so much that justifying my history with a transcontinental region didn't do me…justice? And now, I am in the USA, the land of the free and the home of the brave (quick jingle hum). I graduated from Cleveland State University with a major in Supply chain and a minor in English…hence the formation of this rhythmic collection. Now, I live in Virginia—not long before I move again. The poems you've read inside have conformed the journey of my youth. They are solemn, simple, and hopefully worth every second of your precious time. There's more to come, a lot more. Hope you walk by me as I share more of my words, they will live on in your hearts and minds when one day none of me is left behind.

Printed in Great Britain
by Amazon